Aberdeenshire

COUNCIL

Aberdeenshire Library and Information Service
www.aberdeenshire.gov.uk/libraries
Renewals Hotline 01224 661511

-3 FEB. 2012
(HQ)
- 7 DEC 2011

2 1 DEC 2012
2 8 MAR 2013

19 DEC 2014

HQ

- 3 APR 2015

2 1 DEC 2016

FOOD & HOW TO COOK IT!

MEAT AND FISH

BY CLAIRE LLEWELLYN
WITH RECIPES BY CLARE O'SHEA

WAYLAND

First published in 2009 by Wayland
Copyright © Wayland 2009

Wayland
338 Euston Road
London NW1 3BH

Wayland Australia
Level 17/207 Kent Street
Sydney NSW 2000

Commissioning editor: Jennifer Sanderson
Designer: www.rawshock.co.uk
Photographer: Andy Crawford
Illustrator: Ian Thompson
Hand model: Camilla Lloyd
Proofreader and indexer: Susie Brooks
Consultant: Clare O'Shea - Clare has taught food
technology for more than 17 years in various London-
based schools. She is currently Head of Food Technology
at London Academy, where she teaches years 7 to 13.
The Academy delivers GCSE Hospitality and Catering to
years 10 and 11, A Level Food Technology and the Food
Hygiene Certificate.

British Cataloguing in Publication Data

O'Shea, Clare.
   Meat & fish. -- (Food and how to cook it)
   1. Meat--Juvenile literature.
2. Fish as food--Juvenile literature.
3. Cookery (Meat)--Juvenile literature.
4. Cookery (Fish)--Juvenile literature.
I. Title II. Series III. Llewellyn, Claire.
   641.3'6-dc22

ISBN: 978 0 7502 5661 2

Printed in China

Wayland is a division of Hachette Children's Books,
an Hachette UK company.
www.hachette.co.uk

Picture Acknowledgements:
All photography by Andy Crawford, except: Alan & Sandy
Carey/Getty Images: COVER, 12; Nigel Cattlin/Alamy: 24; Peter
Dazeley/Getty Images: 40B; Natalie Forbes/Corbis: 38; Peter
Frischmuth/argus/Still Pictures: 31; Wayne Hutchinson/Alamy: 6;
iStockphoto.com: 8T & C, 13, 19, 25, 32, 40T Dave King/Getty
Images: 41; Lardi/Andia/Still Pictures: 9; Julian Love Photography/
Alamy: 4; PhotoEdit/Alamy: 30; Helene Rogers/Alamy: 11;
Visuals Unlimited/Corbis: 10

Note:
In preparation of this book, all due care has been exercised with
regard to the advice, activities and techniques depicted. The publishers
regret that they can accept no liability for any loss or injury sustained.

The website addresses (URLs) included in this book were valid at the
time of going to press. However, because of the nature of the Internet,
it is possible that some addresses may have changed, or sites may have
changed or closed down since publication. While the authors and
publishers regret any inconvenience this may cause the readers, no
responsibility for any such changes can be accepted by either the authors
or the publishers.

Contents

Meat, fish and a balanced diet

Meat and fish appear on plates and menus in almost every part of the world. A wide range of animals are farmed or caught for their meat – from fish and shellfish to birds, such as chickens, and larger animals including pigs, cows and sheep.

Doner kebab, a Turkish speciality, is made of layered slices of lamb, cooked on a vertical spit. The sliced meat is added to pitta bread with pickles, salad and a yoghurt sauce.

Food and culture

The food we eat, or our diet, is influenced by many things, such as whether we live in a hot or cold climate, in the mountains or by the sea. For example, people who live in coastal regions often eat more fish and seafood because it is more readily available than meat and chicken. People's diet also depends on their culture and beliefs. Meat and fish are often the core part of a meal – but many people are vegetarians and choose not to eat these products. The way we prepare and eat any food can be an important part of tradition, featuring in family events, national dishes, festivals and ceremonies that vary around the world.

A healthy diet

Our diet is an important part of a healthy lifestyle. There are five main food groups that contain different nutrients that work together to keep the body healthy. These groups are often shown on a 'food plate', where you can see the proportions in which they should be eaten (see page 5). Added to these food groups is water. We need about six to eight glasses of water each day to keep our bodies healthy.

 Meat, poultry, fish and shellfish are excellent forms of protein. Eggs are another protein-rich food, along with plant foods such as pulses, nuts and seeds.

The food plate

Fruit and vegetables: Full of vitamins and minerals, these foods protect our body and reduce the risk of heart disease, stroke and some cancers. The fibre in them helps to bulk up our food and keep our digestive system healthy. Fruit and vegetables are low in fat, so they fill us up without unnecessary calories.

Carbohydrates: These provide us with energy. Starchy carbohydrates, which include grains and cereals, should make up about 30 per cent of the food we eat. Starchy carbohydrates are an important source of energy for sportsmen and women because they release the energy slowly, keeping the body going for longer.

FRUIT AND VEGETABLES

CARBOHYDRATES

PROTEIN

FATS

MILK AND DAIRY

Protein: This builds and repairs our bones, muscles, skin, hair and tissues. Meat, fish, eggs and pulses that provide body-building proteins should make up about 15 per cent of our total daily diet.

Fats: These keep us warm and can also be stored in the body for energy. Foods that are high in saturated fats (fats from animal sources) or sugar, such as cakes, biscuits and crisps, should be eaten only in small amounts (about 8 per cent of our total diet). Fats found in oily fish, olives and nuts and seeds are called unsaturated fats. Saturated fats are linked to an increased risk of heart disease. Eating unsaturated fats is a healthier alternative.

Dairy: Dairy products include milk, butter, yoghurt and cheese. They are packed with nutrients, such as calcium, magnesium, Vitamin K, zinc and protein, and help to build strong bones and teeth. Yoghurt is full of good bacteria and improves our immune system and digestive health. It is best to eat cheese in moderation because it is high in fat.

FOOD FACTS

Eating a moderate amount of protein, in one or two meals every day, will give you all the protein you need for a balanced diet. Here are some examples of a moderate serving of protein:

60–100g boneless meat or poultry
100g fish
2 medium eggs
3 tablespoons of seeds
3 tablespoons of nuts

Meat and poultry are tasty, nutritious foods that are easy to prepare. With their different flavours and cuts, they are very versatile and provide us with a lot of choice.

Which meats?

The most popular meats are beef (from cows), lamb (from sheep) and pork (from pigs). These are all known as red meats. Poultry refers to farmyard birds such as chicken and turkey, and these produce white meats. Other edible birds include duck, pheasant and guinea fowl. Veal (from calves), mutton (from sheep), venison (from deer), rabbit and hare are also eaten.

 In summer, cattle raised for their beef graze on grass. In late autumn, they are taken inside and fed on cereals and silage (conserved grass).

Meat in the diet

Meat and poultry are high in protein, which helps the body to grow and repair itself after injury. These foods are also a good source of vitamins and minerals, especially iron. Iron is important for the body, helping it to form the red blood cells that carry oxygen to every organ. Some cuts of meat can be high in fat, so it is wise to choose leaner cuts and remove any visible fat. The meat from poultry is a good choice because it is lower in fat.

Offal

While the word 'meat' refers to an animal's muscle tissue, the word 'offal' is the name given to any other part of its body. Well-known examples of offal include the brain, liver, kidneys and tongue. Offal is rich in iron and vitamins, but it has a strong flavour and is less popular today than in the past. However, it is still often combined with other meats – for example, in patés or steak and kidney pudding.

How was it farmed?

Meat and poultry may be farmed intensively indoors or 'free range' outdoors. Some people have complained about the conditions on intensive farms. In the United Kingdom (UK) there are strict guidelines to control animal welfare and, whatever its source, all meat is equally nutritious. Check the label to find out how the meat you have bought has been farmed. The label should also tell you if the product is organic, or free from chemical preservatives.

Processing meat

Fresh meat and poultry can be minced and mixed with other ingredients to make sausages, patés and pies.

FOOD FACTS

We do not need a lot of meat in our daily diet. About 60–100g a day is sufficient, eaten with plenty of vegetables and starchy foods, such as rice, noodles or potatoes.

Meat can also be cured to make salami-type sausages, bacon, ham and other processed meats. We should avoid eating too many processed meats because they are high in saturated fats and contain a lot of salt. Too much salt increases the risk of a heart attack or stroke.

What about vegetarians?

Many people choose not to eat meat for religious, ethical or dietary reasons. So where do they find their daily protein? Cheese is high in protein but also high in fat. A better choice are the plant proteins, which include different types of pulses as well as nuts and seeds. Pulses must be combined with grains, seeds or nuts to provide a complete form of protein – for example, in the popular meal of baked beans on toast. These, combined with eggs, dairy products, cereals and rice, will provide all the protein the body needs.

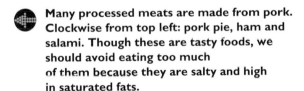

Many processed meats are made from pork. Clockwise from top left: pork pie, ham and salami. Though these are tasty foods, we should avoid eating too much of them because they are salty and high in saturated fats.

It is much healthier to eat lean meat and poultry instead of processed meat. When cooking meat and poultry, cut off any visible fat before you cook it.

From haddock to halibut and pollack to plaice, fish is delicious, healthy and cooks very quickly.

Fish in the diet

Fish is such a healthy food that nutritionists recommended that we try to eat it twice a week. Fish is low in fat, a great source of protein, and contains many vitamins and minerals.

Some kinds of fish are more nutritious than others. Oily fish, such as mackerel and trout, contain oils known as Omega-3 oils. These unsaturated fats help us to think and use our brains well, and lower the risk of heart attacks.

Which fish?

Fish can be sorted into three different groups:

Variety	Fish
Oily fish	Tuna, trout, sardines, mackerel, salmon, herring and fresh tuna are known as oily fish. Oily fish are very healthy because they contain Omega-3 oils.
White fish	Cod, haddock, hake, plaice and sole are among the best-known white fish. They have a delicate flavour and are very low in fat.
Shellfish and other seafood	Prawns, mussels, crabs and lobster are known as shellfish. They contain similar nutrients to white fish and are rich in minerals. Squid (and its cousin, the octopus) is a kind of mollusc. This seafood can be used in many dishes and is high in protein.

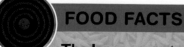

FOOD FACTS

The Japanese eat more fish than any other country. Japan has one of the lowest levels of heart disease in the world.

Mussel farming is a natural process. Baby mussels attach themselves to ropes or poles, take in food as they need it from the water, and are harvested after three years when they are fully grown.

Finding fish

Fish is the world's last great wild food resource. Most of the fish we buy in the shops has been caught in seas and oceans. However, fish stocks are declining, and an increasing amount of certain species, such as salmon, trout, prawns and mussels, are now raised on fish farms. This is known as aquaculture. Fish on fish farms are fed regularly, so they do not have to swim to hunt for food. Due to this lack of exercise, farmed fish have a layer of fat.

Processing fish

Fresh fish is combined with other ingredients to make fish fingers, fishcakes, patés, soups and pies. Fresh fish spoils easily, so much of it is preserved by freezing, drying, salting or smoking. Smoked fish includes kippers (smoked herrings), smoked salmon, smoked trout and smoked mackerel. Fish such as tuna, mackerel and crab meat, can also be preserved in brine, oils or water, and canned. Seafood, such as mussels, can be preserved and sold in bottles or jars.

 Smoked mackerel (left) and canned tuna (right) are two kinds of processed fish. The mackerel contains oils that are good for our health. While fresh tuna also contains these oils, canned tuna does not. This is because the fish is cooked before the canning process.

Handling meat and fish

Before you start to cook with meat or fish, it is important to know about keeping it fresh and safe to eat. Like most foods, meat and fish contain bacteria that can become harmful if you are careless.

Beating bacteria

There are two main types of bacteria – one that makes the food spoil, or 'go off', and one that can cause food poisoning and make you ill. Salmonella, listeria and E coli are just some of the dangerous bacteria you might have heard of. These are examples of bacteria that cause food poisoning. Fortunately, it is easy to destroy these bugs, or stop them from spreading, by storing food at the right temperature, handling it carefully and cooking it in the correct way.

FOOD FACTS

It is not always easy to tell if food is contaminated because often it looks, smells and tastes fine. Symptoms of food poisoning include fever, vomiting, stomach pains and diarrhoea.

Sensible storage

Bacteria thrive at room temperature, so place well-wrapped meat and fish in the fridge or freezer as soon as you return from the shop. Store raw meat and fish at the bottom of a fridge, away from cooked foods, cheese and vegetables, to avoid contamination.

 Handle with care! A greatly magnified view of E coli bacteria, which can cause food poisoning.

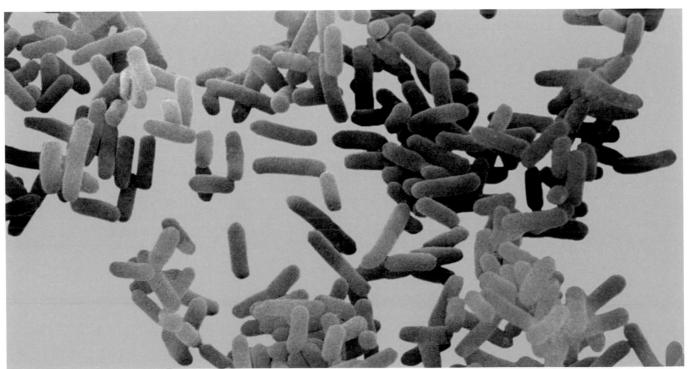

Food	Storage time in a fridge
Raw fish	1 day
Raw meat	2 days
Raw poultry	2 days
Raw offal	1 day
Raw sausages	3 days
Cooked meats	2 days

Careful cooking

Make sure you cook meat and fish thoroughly – it should be searing hot all the way through. With poultry, mince and sausages make sure there is no pink left on the inside. When these meats are fully cooked, the juices should run clear.

Leftovers

If you have cooked meat or fish and are not going to eat it straight away, cool it as quickly as possible and then put it in the fridge or freezer. When you reheat it, make sure it is steaming hot.

Defrosting frozen meat and fish

When meat or fish thaws, a lot of liquid may come out of it. This liquid will spread bacteria onto any food, plate or surface that it touches. Keep meat or fish in a sealed container, preferably at the bottom of the fridge, so that it cannot touch or drip onto other foods. Do not leave it at room temperature, where bacteria will multiply.

If you defrost raw meat or fish and then cook it thoroughly, you can freeze it again – but never reheat foods more than once.

Handling raw foods

Always thoroughly clean plates, utensils, work surfaces and your hands after they have touched raw or thawing meat or fish. This will stop harmful bacteria from spreading. Never let raw meat come into contact with cooked food, or ready-to-eat raw food such as salad vegetables – the bacteria will not be destroyed if the food is not going to be cooked further and could cause food poisoning. Use separate chopping boards for raw meat, poultry and fish.

 To keep food safe, refrigerate! Food should not be left out of the fridge for more than an hour. Put meat and fish in the fridge as soon as you get it home.

Beef

Beef is a dark, nutritious red meat with a deep, rich flavour. It can be used in a huge variety of dishes, including roast dinners, warming stews, cottage pies and spaghetti bolgonese.

Raising beef cattle

Beef cattle are reared all over the world, but especially in places where there is plenty of grazing, such as Australia, Brazil, Argentina and Canada. Most breeds of beef cattle are different from the breeds used for milk. For generations, beef cattle have been bred to grow quickly, producing a lot of meat. They mostly graze in fields during the summer and are kept indoors in winter when the grass has stopped growing. Then they are fed on dried or preserved grass, supplemented with cereals or beans. Beef cattle are slaughtered when they are about 18 months old. After slaughter, the animal is hung for between one and three weeks to give the meat a fuller flavour.

 Some beef farmers rear cattle from birth to slaughter. Others sell their animals on for fattening after 6 to 12 months.

Veal

Veal is the meat of young male dairy cows, which cannot produce milk. It was once unpopular because of poor farm practices, but today this meat is being raised to high welfare standards in many countries, such as the UK. All British animals live outdoors in the summer and feed on natural food. The animals go to slaughter when they are five months old. The tender pink meat is delicately flavoured and contains virtually no fat. Like beef, veal can be roasted or stewed. The best meat is cut into slices and beaten thin to make escalopes. Wiener schnitzel, a well-known Austrian dish, uses escalopes of veal.

Processing beef

Beef is processed in many different ways. The fresh meat can be minced and made into beefburgers or chopped and added to stews and pies. Beef can also be preserved by salting or curing to produce bresaola, pastrami or corned beef, which are sold at the delicatessen counter.

Who eats beef?

Beef is eaten in most parts of the world. The UK is famous for its roast beef served with Yorkshire pudding, while steaks and hamburgers are devoured in North and South America and Australia. Beef is not popular in India, where the cow is sacred to the Hindu religion, or in the Middle East, where people traditionally prefer lamb.

Beefburgers are served in a soft bread roll with a choice of extras, such as lettuce, tomato, onion, pickle, a slice of cheese, mustard, ketchup, mayonnaise, salsa and peppers.

FOOD FACTS

Beefburgers are also known as 'hamburgers'. The name comes from the German city of Hamburg, where sandwiches of hot minced beef used to be very popular. Hamburgers never contain ham!

Cuts of beef

A beef animal's carcass is quartered and cut into various pieces. Each part produces different meat that needs cooking in different ways (see below). Some of the tougher cuts may be put through a mincer. Minced beef is very versatile and can be used in many dishes including meatballs, beefburgers, bolognese sauce or spicy chilli con carne.

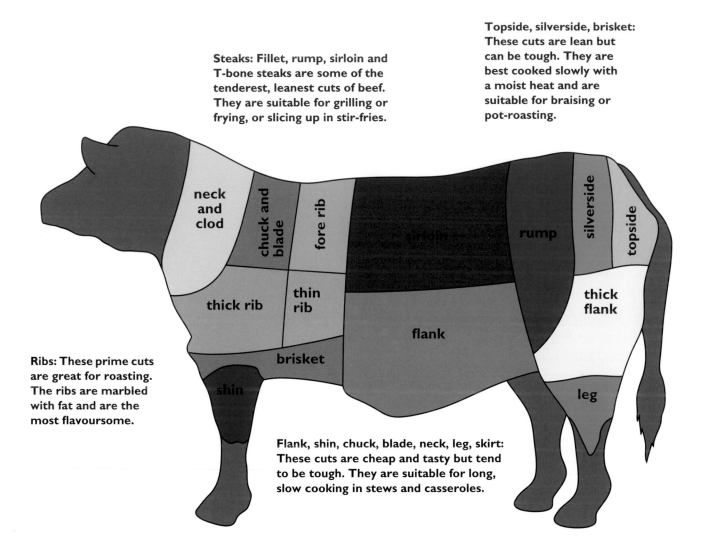

Steaks: Fillet, rump, sirloin and T-bone steaks are some of the tenderest, leanest cuts of beef. They are suitable for grilling or frying, or slicing up in stir-fries.

Topside, silverside, brisket: These cuts are lean but can be tough. They are best cooked slowly with a moist heat and are suitable for braising or pot-roasting.

Ribs: These prime cuts are great for roasting. The ribs are marbled with fat and are the most flavoursome.

Flank, shin, chuck, blade, neck, leg, skirt: These cuts are cheap and tasty but tend to be tough. They are suitable for long, slow cooking in stews and casseroles.

neck and clod

chuck and blade

fore rib

sirloin

silverside

topside

rump

thick rib

thin rib

thick flank

flank

brisket

shin

leg

KNOW YOUR FOOD

Fresh beef has cream-coloured fat and bright red meat. Choose well-trimmed, lean cuts of meat without too much fat. If buying mince, check the fat content and choose the lowest amount for the healthiest option.

Cooking beef

Cooking beef, and other types of meat, makes it more tender and digestible. In addition to cooking, there are various methods to ensure the meat is perfectly prepared before eating. These techniques can be used for other types of meat, too.

FOOD FACTS

Marinading is the process of soaking foods in a seasoned liquid. The ingredients for marinades come from three groups – acids, oils, and seasonings. Acids, such as fruit juice or vinegar, will tenderise meat. Oils lock in its flavour and moisture. Seasonings, such as herbs and garlic, add flavours.

Technique		Description
	Trimming	Trim any fat off the edge of the beef before cooking it so that the cut is leaner and more healthy.
	Scoring	If you score the meat before you marinade it, the marinade will be able to soak right into the cut.
	Marinading	The longer meat is left to soak up marinade, the more flavoursome and tender it will be (see below).

Beef marinade

SERVES: 2   **PREPARATION TIME: 10 MINUTES**   **COOKING TIME: NO COOKING**

If you leave meat overnight in this marinade, it will be lovely and tender when you come to cook it.

Ingredients:
1 garlic clove
15ml soy sauce
juice 1 lime

1. Peel and crush the garlic.

2. Combine the crushed garlic, soy sauce and lime juice.

3. Pour over the meat you want to marinate. If possible, leave the meat to marinate overnight in a sealed container in the fridge.

Lasagne

Lasagne is a traditional Italian 'al forno' pasta dish. Al forno means 'from the oven'.

Ingredients
100g Cheddar cheese, grated
1 tablespoon plain white flour
500ml milk
1 tablespoon vegetable oil
200g minced beef
2 garlic cloves, peeled and finely chopped
1 onion, peeled and finely chopped
400g tin tomatoes
1 tablespoon tomato purée
½ teaspoon sugar
1 beef stock cube
150g dried lasagne sheets

1. Preheat the oven to 200°C/ gas mark 6.

2. To make the cheese sauce, place three-quarters of the Cheddar cheese, plus the flour and milk, in a saucepan over a medium heat. Stir continuously in a figure of eight until the sauce thickens. Remove from the heat

3. To make the meat sauce, heat the oil over a medium heat and fry the beef, garlic and onion until the meat has turned brown and the onions are soft. There should be no pink on the meat.

4. Add the chopped tomatoes, tomato purée and sugar to the meat. Crumble the stock cube into the meat sauce and stir well.

5. Bring the sauce to the boil then turn off the heat.

6. To assemble the lasagne, start with a layer of meat sauce, then a layer of lasagne sheets and some cheese sauce. Repeat until all the meat sauce, pasta and cheese sauce is used up, finishing with a layer of cheese sauce.

7. Sprinkle over the remaining cheese and bake in the oven for 30 minutes until golden brown.

COOK'S TIP

Try using a mixture of cheeses, such as Parmesan and Cheddar.

Burgers

SERVES: 2	PREPARATION TIME: 20 MINUTES	COOKING TIME: 10–12 MINUTES

Originally hamburgers were from Hamburg in Germany. Their popularity has spread and today, people all over the world eat burgers.

Ingredients

300g minced beef
1 small onion, peeled and chopped
salt and pepper
1 egg
1 tablespoon soy sauce
2 soft burger buns
mayonnaise (optional)
tomato ketchup (optional)
1 medium tomato, sliced
6 slices cucumber
4 iceberg lettuce leaves
chips, to serve

1. Put the minced beef, onion, salt, pepper, egg and soy sauce in a bowl and squeeze it together using your fingers.

2. Divide the meat mixture into four equal portions and pat firmly into round burgers.

3. Turn the grill on high and grill the burgers for 6 minutes on each side.

4. In the meantime, prepare the buns. Cut each bun in half and spread mayonnaise to taste on the bottom and ketchup to taste on the top.

5 Add 2 leaves of lettuce, some tomato slices and 3 slices of cucumber to each bun.

6. When the burgers are cooked, add them to the buns. Serve immediately with chips.

Beef and pepper stir-fry

SERVES: 4	PREPARATION TIME: 20 MINUTES	COOKING TIME: 15 MINUTES

Piping hot stir-fries are tasty to eat and quick and easy to make.

Ingredients

300g lean beef
1 garlic clove, peeled and finely chopped
1 tablespoon vegetable oil
1 red pepper
5 pak choi leaves
200ml oyster sauce
2 sachets straight to wok noodles
2 tablespoons cold water

1. Slice the beef into strips about 1cm wide.

2. Put the beef and garlic into a wok or large frying pan with the oil and set aside.

3. Deseed and slice the red pepper into strips, about 5mm wide. Slice the pak choi into strips about 1cm wide.

4. Fry the beef and garlic over a medium heat until there is no pink left on the meat.

5. Add the oyster sauce and stir well.

6. Add the peppers and pak choi and cook for 5 minutes, stirring all the time.

7. Add the noodles and water and cook for another 5 minutes. Serve piping hot.

Lamb

Lamb is a tender, delicious red meat that is eaten all over the world. It is ideal for a variety of dishes, including barbequed kebabs, roasts and stews.

Breeding sheep

Sheep are hardy animals. They can be kept outdoors for much of the year, grazing on rough ground. Breeds are chosen to suit the climate and land – for example, tough, sure-footed sheep are selected for places with a harsh climate and rugged terrain. The sheep are often allowed to roam over large areas so that they can find enough food to survive. In many upland areas they are brought down into valleys in the winter, for protection from the bitter weather. On better grassland, sheep have been cross-bred, resulting in animals with useful characteristics. They are strong, look after their young, and give birth to plenty of fast-growing lambs that provide excellent quality meat.

Rearing lambs

Most lambs are born in early spring when the grass is starting to grow. They suckle from their mothers at first, then gradually begin feeding on pasture or hay and cereal feed. The young

Exporters

Producers

 This map shows the main producers and exporters of lamb.

Lamb tagine is a tasty, slow-cooked dish from Morocco. The word 'tagine' refers to the cone-shaped cooking dish in which the stew is cooked.

animals are separated from their mothers when they are four months old. They go to slaughter throughout the summer. The younger the animal, the more tender its meat.

Older mutton

Mutton is the name given to the meat of a sheep over one year old. Mutton is darker and has a stronger flavour than lamb. The meat is tougher and needs longer, slower cooking, making it suitable for hot-pots, curries and casseroles.

Who eats lamb?

Lamb is a familiar meat in most parts of the world. In Greece, a whole lamb is roasted very slowly to make a popular dish called kleftiko. Lamb is also minced and combined with aubergines to make the dish moussaka. In North Africa, lamb tagines are made from stewed lamb and are often served with couscous (a grainy dish made from crushed wheat), while lamb kebabs are popular throughout the Middle East. The Indians add lamb to curries, and it also forms the base to traditional British dishes such as Lancashire hot-pot and shepherd's pie.

FOOD FACTS

Some shepherds keep mixed flocks of sheep and goats. Goat is eaten instead of lamb in parts of Europe, Central and South America, Pakistan, India and the Far East. Curried goat is popular in Jamaica.

Cuts of lamb

Lamb is a red meat, though the younger the animal, the paler its meat. The carcass is cut into various pieces, which need to be prepared in different ways. Some cuts, such as the leg, can be roasted, while chops can be quickly grilled or fried. Other cuts, such as lamb shank, need many hours of slow cooking until the meat is meltingly tender and almost falling off the bone. Minced lamb is delicately flavoured and can be used in dozens or ways – for example to make meatballs or in a stuffing for peppers or other vegetables.

KNOW YOUR FOOD

Choose well-trimmed, lean cuts of meat without too much fat. Lamb meat should be pink, and its fat firm and creamy white. For mutton, choose meat with a rich brown colour. If you're buying mince, check the fat content and go for the lowest amount.

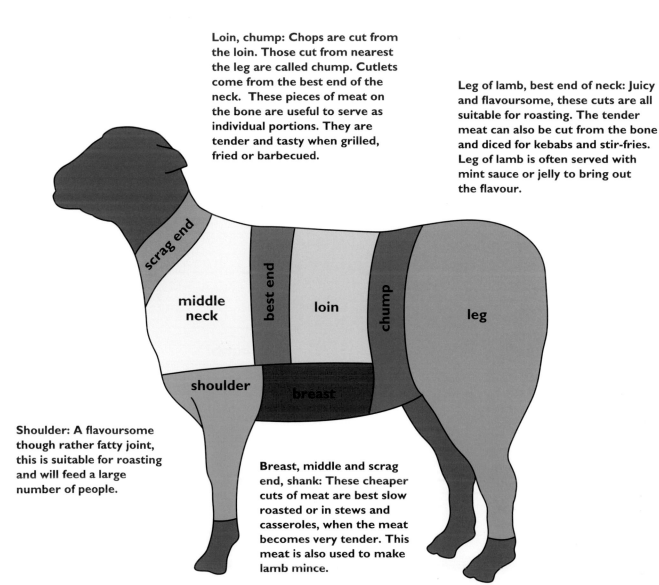

Loin, chump: Chops are cut from the loin. Those cut from nearest the leg are called chump. Cutlets come from the best end of the neck. These pieces of meat on the bone are useful to serve as individual portions. They are tender and tasty when grilled, fried or barbecued.

Leg of lamb, best end of neck: Juicy and flavoursome, these cuts are all suitable for roasting. The tender meat can also be cut from the bone and diced for kebabs and stir-fries. Leg of lamb is often served with mint sauce or jelly to bring out the flavour.

Shoulder: A flavoursome though rather fatty joint, this is suitable for roasting and will feed a large number of people.

Breast, middle and scrag end, shank: These cheaper cuts of meat are best slow roasted or in stews and casseroles, when the meat becomes very tender. This meat is also used to make lamb mince.

scrag end

middle neck

best end

loin

chump

leg

shoulder

breast

Moussaka

SERVES: 2 | **PREPARATION TIME: 30 MINUTES** | **COOKING TIME: 30 MINUTES**

Moussaka is a traditional Greek dish of lamb mince, aubergines and a cheese sauce.

Ingredients
1 large aubergine, stalk removed
  and sliced
salt
4 tablespoons olive oil
400g minced lamb
1 onion, peeled and finely chopped
2 garlic cloves, peeled and finely
  chopped
400g tin tomatoes
1 tablespoon tomato purée
1 teaspoon dried oregano
1 beef stock cube
50g grated Cheddar cheese
250ml milk
1 tablespoon plain white flour
Greek salad, to serve

1. Preheat the oven to 180°C/ gas mark 6.

2. Sprinkle salt onto the aubergine slices and leave them to stand for 15 minutes. Rinse them under cold running water and pat dry with kitchen towel.

3. Heat one-third of the oil in a frying pan over a medium heat and fry one-third of the aubergines until slightly brown. Repeat until all the aubergines are done. Set them aside until later.

4. Fry the lamb, onion and garlic until brown. Add the tomatoes, tomato purée, oregano and the stock cube. Stir well and bring to the boil. Leave to simmer for about 20 minutes.

5. In the meantime, make the cheese sauce. Put the cheese, milk and flour into a saucepan and stir constantly in a figure of eight over a medium heat until the sauce thickens.

6. Put the meat sauce in a large ovenproof dish, lay the fried aubergine slices on top and cover with the cheese sauce.

7. Bake for 30 minutes. When ready, cut into portions and serve with Greek salad.

COOK'S TIP

To make a Greek salad, combine cucumber slices, cherry tomatoes, feta cheese and black olives. Drizzle with olive oil.

Shepherd's pie

SERVES: 4   PREPARATION TIME: 20 MINUTES   COOKING TIME: 30 MINUTES

This English lamb dish is sometimes cooked with minced beef and called cottage pie.

Ingredients
4 medium potatoes
1 tablespoon vegetable oil
200g minced lamb
1 small onion, peeled and
   finely chopped
400g tin vegetable soup
3 tablespoons milk
1 tablespoon butter
50g Cheddar cheese, grated

1. Preheat the oven to 180°C/gas mark 4.

2. To make the mashed potato, half fill a medium-sized saucepan with water and place it over a medium heat to boil. Peel and cut each potato into four pieces. Place the potato pieces in the boiling water and allow to boil for 20 minutes, until soft.

3. In the meantime, heat the oil in a large frying pan and fry the mince and onion until the meat is brown.

4. Add the vegetable soup and leave it to simmer for 15 minutes.

5. When the potatoes are soft, turn off the heat, drain them and put them back in the saucepan. Add the milk and butter and mash until smooth (see page 47).

6. Place the meat mixture in a medium-sized ovenproof dish and spread the potato mash on top.

7. Run a fork along the mash to create lines and top with the grated cheese.

8. Bake in the oven for 20 minutes until golden brown.

Lamb curry

SERVES: 2 | **PREPARATION TIME: 20 MINUTES** | **COOKING TIME: 30 MINUTES**

This Indian curry is delicious served with rice. You can add more heat, if you like, by adding chillies.

Ingredients
200g lean lamb, cubed
1 tablespoon oil
1 small onion
100g tikka masala curry paste
200ml natural yoghurt
75g basmati rice
small bunch fresh coriander

1. Place the lamb in a saucepan with the oil. Set aside.

2. Peel and finely chop the onion. Add it to the lamb.

3. To cook the rice, put 125ml of water on to boil.

4. In the meantime, cook the lamb and onion over a medium heat until the meat is brown.

5. Add the curry paste and stir well. Stir in the yoghurt and leave to simmer for 30 minutes.

6. Add the rice to the boiling water and cook for about 20 minutes until all the water has been absorbed.

7. When the curry is cooked, sprinkle with coriander leaves and serve with the rice.

Shish kebabs

SERVES: 4 | **PREPARATION TIME: 20 MINUTES** | **COOKING TIME: 10 MINUTES**

This Turkish dish has been adopted the world over and is especially popular in Greece.

Ingredients
500g lean lamb, cubed
1 onion
50g red cabbage, sliced
2 tomatoes, sliced
4 pitta breads
bunch fresh coriander

For the marinade
3 tablespoons olive oil
juice 1 lemon
2 garlic cloves, peeled and chopped
salt and pepper

1. Mix all of the ingredients for the marinade in a bowl. Put the lamb into the marinade, cover the bowl with cling film and leave it in the fridge for about 1 hour.

2. In the meantime, cut the onion into chunks and set aside.

3. When the meat is ready, divide the onion and meat into four equal portions. Thread each portion onto a metal skewer, starting with a piece of lamb, then some onion, then some lamb. Continue until it is all used up.

4. Place the skewers under a hot grill for about 10 minutes, turning all the time, until the meat is cooked.

5. While the meat is cooking, toast the pitta breads until they puff up. Slice them lengthways to open.

6. Fill each pitta bread with cabbage and tomato and serve with the warm kebabs.

Pork

Pork is a flavoursome, nutritious meat that can be eaten in many ways. It is used to make many delicious foods such as sausages, ham and bacon.

Raising pigs

Contrary to what many people think, pigs are clean, intelligent animals. Traditionally they were raised in woodland areas, where they fed on acorns.

Today, most pigs are reared indoors. The animals are kept in groups in pens, but give birth in a separate farrowing house on individual farrowing crates. This is to protect the tiny piglets from being crushed by their super-sized mum. The piglets leave the sow (female pig) after a month, and are then fed a carefully balanced diet so that they grow quickly and produce a lot of lean meat. Most pigs are slaughtered by the time they are six months old, when they weigh up to 100 kilograms.

Free-range pigs display natural instincts such as rooting in the soil. As they are more active than indoor-reared pigs, they grow at a slower rate, so their meat becomes more flavoursome and succulent.

Free range pigs

Some pigs are raised free range. Sturdier, fatter breeds are chosen for this because the animals must survive outdoors in all weathers. The sows are fed similar diets to animals kept indoors, but they also graze on grass. They need more food than indoor pigs because they use more energy roaming around. In summer, the pigs are given wallows of water to help them keep cool, as well as shade so that they are not burnt by the sun. The pigs sleep in huts with straw bedding and give birth to their litters in individual shelters.

How is pork eaten?

Fresh pork can be prepared in many different ways. The best cuts of meat can be roasted whole or thinly sliced and cooked in stir-fries. Fattier cuts of meat need gentle roasting or braising. Fresh pork can also be put through a mincer to provide minced pork (also known as ground pork). This can then be used in stuffings for vegetables or mixed with breadcrumbs, onions, herbs and spices to make tasty meatballs. Turkeys cooked at Christmas are sometimes stuffed with a mixture of pork and herbs.

Fresh pork can also be processed. It is used in patés and to make sausages. It is also preserved as gammon, bacon and ham and is an ingredient in salami-type sausages, Scotch eggs and pork pies. These preserved and processed meats were originally created as long-lasting foods before fridges were invented. They are still popular because of their flavour, though we should avoid eating too many of them because they are often high in salt and fat.

Who eats pork?

Meat eaters all around the world eat pork, with the exception of Muslims and Jews who consider pigs to be unclean. Pork is very popular in China, where it is added to stir-fries or used to make sweet and sour pork, soups and spring rolls. In the UK, pork is traditionally served with apple sauce or enjoyed as bacon with eggs for breakfast. Other famous pork dishes include pork and beans, which is eaten in Brazil and Portugal, and sticky spare ribs, which are eaten in the southern USA. Hot dogs are a favourite food and are eaten almost everywhere in the world – most famously at baseball games in the USA. The traditional spicy frankfurter sausage is often made from a combination of meats, including beef and pork.

KNOW YOUR FOOD

If you are looking for lower fat bacon, buy back bacon instead of the streaky kind.

 Hot dogs were one of the world's first 'fast foods'. They are served in a long bread roll, often with a helping of fried onions, mustard or tomato ketchup.

Cuts of pork

Although pork is lighter in colour than beef or lamb, it is still termed a red meat. As with beef and lamb, the animal's carcass is cut into different pieces, or cuts – big joints, lean fillets, chops, and so on. These cuts vary greatly and you can make the best of them by using different cooking methods. Almost every part of the pig can be eaten, including the trotters, ears and even the tail! The colour of pork should be velvety mid-pink and the fat should be firm and white with skin that is dry and silky.

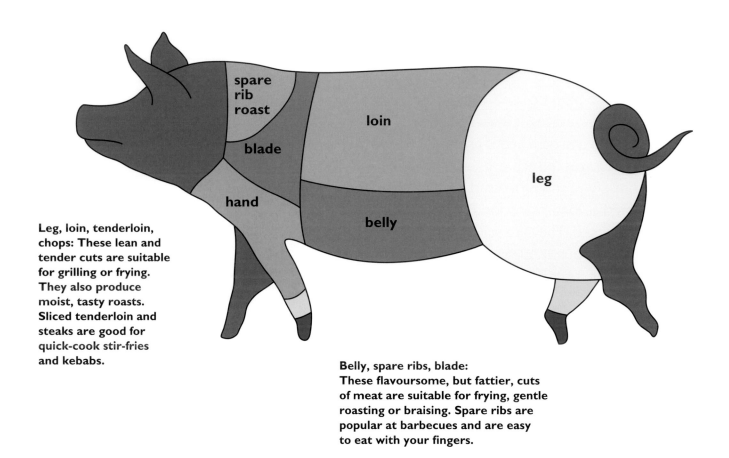

spare rib roast

blade

hand

loin

belly

leg

Leg, loin, tenderloin, chops: These lean and tender cuts are suitable for grilling or frying. They also produce moist, tasty roasts. Sliced tenderloin and steaks are good for quick-cook stir-fries and kebabs.

Belly, spare ribs, blade: These flavoursome, but fattier, cuts of meat are suitable for frying, gentle roasting or braising. Spare ribs are popular at barbecues and are easy to eat with your fingers.

KNOW YOUR FOOD

Before roasting, the layer of fat on the outside of pork can be scored with a sharp knife. It then crisps up to make delicious crackling. Eat it only as a treat as it is very high in fat!

Sweet and sour pork

SERVES: 2 | **PREPARATION TIME: 20 MINUTES** | **COOKING TIME: 15–20 MINUTES**

This dish is a wonderful mix of flavours. It is usually served with rice, but can be served with noodles, too.

Ingredients
300g lean pork
1 small piece fresh ginger
1 tablespoon vegetable oil
227g tin pineapple chunks

For the sauce
2 tablespoons vinegar
1 tablespoon soy sauce
1 tablespoon tomato purée
1 tablespoon brown sugar
200ml cold water
1 level teaspoon corn flour

1. Cut the pork into cubes. Cut the ginger as finely as possible.

2. Heat the oil in a saucepan over a medium heat. Add the pork and ginger and cook until brown.

3. In the meantime, to make the sauce, mix all the sauce ingredients together.

4. When the meat is cooked, add the sauce and pineapple and stir well. Cook for 5 minutes.

5. Serve immediately.

COOK'S TIP

You can use chicken for this dish instead of pork.

Barbecue spare ribs

SERVES: 4 | **PREPARATION TIME: 20 MINUTES** | **COOKING TIME: 1 HOUR**

These mouthwatering ribs are perfect for a summer barbecue served with a salad.

Ingredients
1 tablespoon vegetable oil
1 small onion, peeled and
  finely chopped
1 garlic clove, peeled and
  finely chopped
600g spare ribs
salad, to serve

For the sauce
2 tablespoons tomato purée
4 tablespoons malt vinegar
pinch chilli powder
3 tablespoons honey
1 beef stock cube
150ml water

1. Preheat the oven to 180°C/gas mark 4.

2. Heat the oil in a frying pan over a medium heat. Fry the onion and garlic until the onion changes colour but does not turn brown.

3. Add all the sauce ingredients and stir well. Cook for 10 minutes.

4. Use a pastry brush to spread the sauce all over the ribs.

5. Bake in the oven for 50 minutes, turning occasionally to ensure even cooking. Serve with a salad.

Danish frikadeller

SERVES: 2   **PREPARATION TIME: 20 MINUTES**   **COOKING TIME: 12 MINUTES**

This dish of meatballs is originally from Denmark. It is delicious served with boiled potatoes and cooked red cabbage.

Ingredients
1 small onion
1 garlic clove
250g minced pork
1 egg, beaten
1 tablespoon plain flour
1 tablespoon milk
2 tablespoons vegetable oil
salt and pepper
boiled potatoes, to serve
cooked red cabbage, to serve

1. Peel and finely chop the onion and garlic.

2. Put the onion, garlic and all the other ingredients, except the oil, in a bowl. Squeeze them together with your hands to mix them well.

3. Roll the mixture into 6 equal balls and flatten each one to make an oval-shaped meatball.

4. Heat the oil in a large frying pan over a medium heat. Add the meatballs and fry for 6 minutes. Turn them over and cook the other side for 6 minutes.

5. When cooked, remove the meatballs from the pan and place them on some kitchen towel to absorb any excess oil.

6. Serve with boiled potates and cooked red cabbage.

COOK'S TIP

These meatballs are great eaten cold in a sandwich.

Thai pork with orange

SERVES: 4 | **PREPARATION TIME: 20 MINUTES** | **COOKING TIME: 15 MINUTES**

The citrus flavour from the oranges goes really well with the pork in this Thai recipe.

Ingredients
1 large orange
350g lean pork steak
1 tablespoon vegetable oil
1 garlic clove, peeled and finely chopped
25g peanuts, finely chopped
1 tablespoon soy sauce
grated rind 1 orange
half teaspoon paprika
salt and pepper
lettuce leaves, to serve

1. Peel the orange, making sure you remove as much of the pith as possible. Cut the orange into segments.

2. Cut each segment into 2 pieces and set aside.

3. Remove any fat from the pork and cut it into strips.

4. Heat the oil over a medium heat and fry the pork and garlic until lightly coloured all over.

5. Stir in the peanuts and cook for 1 minute.

6. Add the remaining ingredients, except for the lettuce, and stir well.

7. To serve, put the pork on top of the lettuce leaves and pour over the pan juices.

COOK'S TIP

Lemon or lime can be used for a more zesty flavour.

Chicken and other poultry

Farmyard birds, such as chicken and turkey, are known as poultry. They are popular in everyday meals, as well as at celebrations, and are an excellent low-fat source of protein.

Breeding and hatching

While some chickens are bred for their eggs, those chickens bred for their meat are known as broilers. Most farmers use fast-growing breeds that are strong and healthy and provide plenty of meat. The eggs are hatched in special hatcheries and the day-old chicks are then transported to rearing farms.

Indoors or outdoors

The young birds are raised in different ways. Some are farmed intensively indoors in large, temperature-controlled houses. These conditions are highly specialised and result in the birds growing so quickly that they are ready to go to market in less than 40 days. Some people think that this kind of farming is cruel.

Free-range birds are raised outdoors, where they have access to light, and may have more room to flap their wings and scratch for food. Birds raised on the best poultry farms enjoy total freedom.

 These chickens are being raised intensively: indoors, in crowded conditions, and without natural light so that they are constantly feeding.

Food and slaughter

The birds are fed on cereals mixed with soya and pulses. Some chickens have names that reflect their diet. For example, corn-fed chickens have yellow flesh and are widely considered to have more flavour than birds fed on soya. Intensively reared birds are slaughtered at about 5–6 weeks, free-range birds at about 8 weeks and organic birds at about 10–11 weeks. After slaughter, the best birds are hung for several days, allowing their natural flavours to develop.

Turkeys are reared for about 20 weeks. Free-range and organic birds have a better taste because they are given more time to mature. Their meat is leaner and less fatty than an intensively reared bird.

FOOD FACTS

As a white meat, poultry is a healthy choice because it is lower in saturated fat than red meat. However, it does have fatty skin. The skin keeps the meat moist during cooking, but it is best to avoid eating it.

 Free-range turkeys can roam at will and are given plenty of time to grow. This produces a better tasting meat.

Processed poultry

Chicken and turkey can be bought fresh or ready prepared. Some poultry meat is covered in breadcrumbs and sold as goujons, or kievs stuffed with garlic-flavoured butter. Chicken 'nuggets' are formed from cheaper meat and skin and can be high in fat. Chicken meat is also used in patés, pies, soups and countless ready meals.

 A roast turkey with all the trimmings is the traditional Christmas dinner. Roast goose, a fattier meat, is sometimes eaten, too.

Who eats poultry?

Poultry is so easy to keep that it is raised and eaten all over the world. It is particularly popular in cultures that reject beef or pork. Famous chicken dishes include roast chicken, chicken soup and chicken pie. In India, tandoori chicken and chicken tikka are popular, while chicken satay is eaten throughout South-East Asia. Perhaps the world's most famous poultry dish is the roast turkey eaten for Thanksgiving Day in the USA and throughout the Christian world at Christmas.

Poultry cuts

After slaughter, poultry birds are plucked, gutted, cleaned and bagged. They are either sold whole or cut into portions. A whole bird is good value for money because it provides the basis for several meals. For example, a chicken can be roasted as part of a roast dinner, then the leftovers used in a stir-fry or salad. Finally, the carcass may be boiled with vegetables to make stock for a soup. Both turkey and chicken are available minced. This is a low-fat alternative to mince made from pork, lamb or beef.

• Whole birds

Whole birds can be roasted or boiled. Younger birds are more tender than older ones, so they are best for roasting. Older, tougher birds are better boiled. The meat can then be stripped and used in pies, stews or soups.

FOOD FACTS

Chicken is the world's most popular meat. In the UK alone, 750 million chickens are consumed every year and many people eat chicken up to three times a week.

• Chicken portions

Pre-prepared portions of chicken and turkey are very convenient because they are small and cook more quickly than a whole bird. Only the best parts of the bird – the breasts, legs and wings – are sold in this way.

• Breasts

The breast portions provide the most white meat. This meat is lean and very versatile. It can be eaten whole or cut into strips or cubes. Breast meat is good for kebabs or stir-fries. It does not have a lot of taste, but quickly takes on the flavour of other ingredients if you marinate or spice it before cooking.

• Legs

A leg can be bought as a single piece of meat or separated into the fleshier thigh and the narrow drumstick. Leg meat is darker, fattier and more flavoursome than breast meat. It can be roasted, grilled, poached or fried. The thighs are also good for slower cooking. Drumsticks are often cooked on barbeques because they are easy to eat in your fingers.

• Wings

The wings contain little meat but they are delicious roasted or cooked on a barbeque. Wings should be eaten in moderation because they are high in fat.

KNOW YOUR FOOD

When buying poultry, choose a well-wrapped, undamaged bird with firm, plump flesh. It should have no smell whatsoever.

Buying a whole chicken is economical because it can be used to make several different meals. The best parts of the chicken are also sold as portions. They are: the breast (1); the wings (2) and the legs (3), which are sometimes called drumsticks.

Chicken chop suey

SERVES: 2 | **PREPARATION TIME: 30 MINUTES** | **COOKING TIME: 15 MINUTES**

This Chinese dish is quick and easy and full of flavour. You can eat it with rice or noodles, or on its own.

Ingredients
1 boneless, skinless chicken breast
1 tablespoon vegetable oil
1 small cube fresh ginger
1 garlic clove
3 spring onions
1 medium carrot
4 mushrooms
Chinese leaves
2 tablespoons soy sauce
100g bean sprouts

1. Cut the chicken breast into strips and place it in a wok with the oil. Set aside.

2. Prepare the garlic, ginger and vegetables. Peel the garlic and ginger and chop them both finely.

3. Cut the dark green top off the spring onions and slice the bulb.

4. Peel and slice the carrot into strips. Slice the mushrooms and shred the Chinese leaves.

5. Fry the chicken with the soy sauce, garlic and ginger until there is no pink meat left.

6. Add all the vegetables, including the bean sprouts, and cook for 5 minutes, stirring all the time. Serve immediately.

COOK'S TIP

You can add water chestnuts, bamboo shoots or cashew nuts for extra flavour and crunch.

Barbecue drumsticks

SERVES: 2 | **PREPARATION TIME: 15 MINUTES** | **COOKING TIME: 20 MINUTES**

These drumsticks are delicious cooked under a grill or on a barbecue.

Ingredients
4 chicken drumsticks
2 tablespoons tomato ketchup
2 tablespoons light soy sauce
2 teaspoons honey
I tablespoon sunflower oil
I tablespoon lemon juice
½ teaspoon Chinese
    five spice
salad, to serve

I. Use a sharp knife to make 2–3 gashes on top of each drumstick.

2. Put the tomato ketchup, soy sauce, honey, oil, lemon juice and spice into a container and mix well.

3. Add the drumsticks, making sure they are coated in the marinade. Leave in the fridge for 2 hours.

4. Preheat the grill to a high heat. Place the chicken under the grill, reserving the marinade. Lower the heat to medium and grill the chicken for 5 minutes.

5. Remove the chicken from the grill and, using a pastry brush, coat the drumsticks with the marinade. Turn the drumsticks over to ensure even cooking. Return the chicken to the grill for another 5 minutes before brushing and turning again. Grill for another 10 minutes.

6. Serve straight from the grill with a side salad.

Malay-style chicken

SERVES: 4 | **PREPARATION TIME: 30 MINUTES** | **COOKING TIME: 25–30 MINUTES**

The combination of fruit and chicken in a rich coconut sauce is irresistible. Serve this dish with plain boiled rice for a hearty main meal.

Ingredients
I vegetable stock cube
250ml boiling water
I green pepper
I red pepper
450g chicken meat (breast
    or thighs)
I tablespoon vegetable oil
I teaspoon ground cumin
    I teaspoon ground coriander
        I teaspoon turmeric
            I large onion, peeled
                and sliced
                I garlic clove, peeled and
                    finely chopped
            50g creamed coconut
        250g pineapple, chopped

I. Mix the vegetable stock cube into the water and set aside.

2. Deseed and chop the peppers.

3. Cut the chicken into cubes.

4. Heat the oil over a medium heat and add the spices, onion, garlic, chicken and peppers. Fry for 2-3 minutes.

5. Add the stock, creamed coconut and pineapple, mix well and bring to the boil. Turn down the heat and allow to simmer for 25 minutes. Serve in bowls.

Chicken risotto

This recipe uses long-grain rice but Italians usually use arborio rice. They cook this until it is 'al dente', which means slightly hard to bite.

Ingredients
600ml boiling water
1 chicken stock cube
1 garlic clove
1 boneless, skinless chicken breast
1 tablespoon vegetable oil
1 tablespoon soy sauce
1 small onion
75g long-grain rice
50g frozen peas
50g frozen sweetcorn

1. Add the stock cube to the boiling water and set aside.

2. Peel and finely chop the garlic. Set aside.

3. Cut the chicken into bite-sized cubes and put it into a large saucepan with the oil.

4. Add the garlic and soy sauce to the chicken and stir well.

5. Fry the chicken over a medium heat until there is no pink left on it.

6. In the meantime, peel and finely chop the onion.

7. Add the rice and onion to the chicken and fry for 2 minutes. Add the stock to the chicken and stir well.

8. Add the peas and sweetcorn to the chicken and cook on high until all the water has been absorbed. Serve piping hot.

COOK'S TIP

You can use turkey breasts instead of chicken breasts.

Turkey breasts in orange sauce

SERVES: 4 **PREPARATION TIME: 30 MINUTES** **COOKING TIME: 40 MINUTES**

This turkey dish can also be served with rice or a side helping of carrots and green beans.

Ingredients
2 tablespoons black pepper
1 teaspoon dried oregano
2 garlic cloves, peeled and finely chopped
½ teaspoon ground cumin
125ml orange juice
1 tablespoon honey
2 tablespoons olive oil
1kg skinless, boneless turkey breast
boiled new potatoes, to serve

1. Preheat the oven to 200°C/gas mark 6.

2. To make a marinade, mix the pepper, oregano, garlic cumin, orange juice, honey and oil together to make a paste.

3. Put the turkey breasts in a bowl and pour over the marinade. Cover with cling film and leave in the fridge for 10 minutes.

4. Take the turkey out of the marinade and place it on a baking tray. Bake for 25 minutes.

5. Place the remaining marinade in a saucepan and allow it to simmer until reduced.

6. When the turkey is cooked, cut each breast into thick slices, pour over the sauce and serve with the potatoes.

Chicken soup

SERVES: 4 **PREPARATION TIME: 25 MINUTES** **COOKING TIME: 35–40 MINUTES**

The combination of chicken and pasta makes this a delicious, hearty soup – perfect for a winter's day.

Ingredients
600ml boiling water
half an uncooked chicken
1 small onion, peeled and finely chopped
2 carrots, peeled and diced
2 sticks celery, chopped
1 vegetable stock cube
100g dried pasta
1 tablespoon butter
salt and pepper

1. Put the water into a large saucepan and bring to the boil.

2. Add the chicken to the boiling water, with the onion, carrots and celery, and boil for 20 minutes.

3. Remove the chicken from the water, leaving the soup to simmer.

4. Remove the skin and bones from the chicken and cut up the meat into small pieces. Return the meat to the soup.

5. Add the stock cube, pasta and butter and bring to the boil. Turn down the heat and allow the soup to simmer for 20 minutes. Check that there is enough liquid in the soup, adding more as it cooks, if required.

6. Season to taste and serve.

Fish and shellfish

A huge variety of animals live in the sea – from giant tuna to tiny sprats and shrimps. They make light, quick, healthy meals and are a prime source of quality protein.

How and where are fish caught?

Fish are caught all over the world, in freshwater rivers and lakes and in the sea. Fishing is tough, sometimes dangerous, work. Some fishing boats are small and stay close to the coast, using nets and lines. The fish are gutted by hand on board, packed in ice and brought back to market. Then they are sold by auction.

Other fishing boats are like floating factories, remaining at sea for several weeks. They use enormous nets to trawl the seabed. The huge catch is gutted and frozen before the boats reach land, where the fish is sold at market.

Fish farming

As wild fish stocks are declining, there has been a growth in fish farming (aquaculture). About one-third of seafood is currently produced by fish farms. Fish such as salmon, sea bass, cod and halibut are raised in hatcheries and then reared in cages in the sea. Trout are raised in tanks near rivers.

Shellfish farms include prawns raised in estuaries in tropical waters and mussels reared on ropes attached to rafts. Other species farmed in the UK include oysters, scallops, cockles and clams.

 This huge catch of pollack has been pulled up by trawlers in the Bering Sea, off the coast of Alaska. With many fish species at dangerously low levels, fish farming is a growing industry.

Conserving stocks

There are certain times in the year when you cannot buy a particular kind of fish unless it is frozen. Fish need to breed or they will die out. When they are ready to lay their eggs, female fish have thousands of tiny eggs called roe in their bodies. If they are caught before they have had time to release the eggs into the sea, then there will be no new fish and the numbers of fish in the sea will be fewer.

FOOD FACTS

Fresh and frozen tuna and other oily fish is rich in Omega-3 and -6 oils, which are important for healthy hearts and digestion. We should try to eat one portion of oily fish a week.

Preserving fish

Fish is a highly perishable food, but it can be preserved in a number of ways, including freezing, salting, pickling, smoking and canning.

- In salting, the fish is packed in layers of salt until all of the liquid has drained away. Salt cod is very popular in Spain.
- In pickling, fish is soaked in vinegar and herbs. Scandinavian fresh herring fillets are preserved in this way and are known as rollmops.

- Smoking fish improves its flavour and texture. Some smoked fish, such as kippers, need cooking. Others, such as salmon or mackerel, do not.
- Canning suits oily fish, such as tuna, as well as seafood, such as crab. Anchovies are filleted, salted and packed in oil. Salmon, sardines and tuna are canned in brine, spring water, oil or a tomato sauce.

Raw prawns, when shelled, are grey in colour (left). The flesh turns a pale pink when the prawns are cooked (right).

Fish and chips is a traditional English dish. It is at its best when eaten on the coast, where the fish is always fresh.

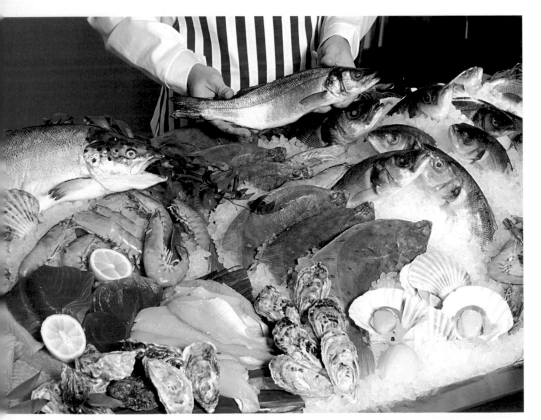

This display of fresh fish and shellfish includes salmon, tuna, plaice, scallops and oysters. The food is displayed on a bed of crushed ice, in order to preserve it.

Who eats fish?

Fish is eaten all over the world, particularly in coastal areas and near rivers and lakes. The world's greatest fish eaters are the Japanese, who eat fish nearly every day. Fish is also very popular in Iceland, Scandinavia and countries around the Mediterranean Sea.

Famous fish dishes include fish and chips, which is eaten in the UK, a fish soup called chowder, which is popular in the USA, and a stew called bouillabaisse, which is eaten in France. In Spain, a fish-and-rice dish called paella is popular and in the Far East, fish curry is regularly made.

Buying fish

Because fish perishes easily, it has to be transported quickly in refrigerated trains and trucks. In shops it is usually displayed on a bed of crushed ice to keep it chilled. All fresh fish must be eaten promptly on the day you buy it. Ideally, it should be eaten within two or three days of being caught.

When buying fish, choose fresh-looking, moist, shiny fish with bright eyes, firm flesh and a clean smell. Smoked fish should look glossy. If buying prepacked fish, always check the sell-by date.

Fish cuts

Fresh fish is usually sold whole. Larger species, such as cod, hake and salmon, are also cut up and sold in fillets or steaks. All fish, whether whole or in pieces, can be poached, steamed, grilled, fried or roasted in the oven. Fish can also be used to make soups, fishcakes, stews and pies. A lot of fish and shellfish is sold frozen. This is convenient because it has usually been cleaned and so there is no or little waste.

• Whole fish

Whole fish are cleaned by gutting – in other words, they are slit open and all the inner organs are removed. The head may also be removed. The fish are then washed under running water. The bones and organs in a fish can amount to more than half of its weight.

• Fillets

In a filleted fish, the flesh has been taken off the bones. This results in long, thin pieces that are easy to eat and can be cooked very quickly.

• Steaks

Steaks are slices of whole fish, usually cut across the bone. The thicker the steak, the longer it will take to cook.

 Fish can be eaten whole on the bone or in smaller portions such as fillets and steaks. From top:
1 Whole trout
2 Fillets of sole
3 Sliced salmon fillets
4 Cod steak
5 Haddock fillet

FOOD FACTS

Nutritionists recommend that we eat two portions of fish a week, one of which should be oil-rich.
Here are some examples of a portion of fish:
1 medium-sized fillet of white fish
1 medium-sized fresh mackerel
1 drained tin of tuna or salmon
6 fish fingers
2 small tins of mackerel or sardines

Garlic prawns

SERVES: 2 | PREPARATION TIME: 5 MINUTES | COOKING TIME: 10 MINUTES

This dish makes a lovely starter – it is full of flavour but light enough to get your tastebuds going before a main meal.

Ingredients

2 garlic cloves, peeled and finely chopped
1 tablespoon butter
10 uncooked prawns
1 tablespoon parsley, chopped

1. Place the butter, garlic and prawns in a frying pan and cook over a medium heat for four minutes on each side. The prawns will turn a light pink when cooked.

2. Remove the pan from the heat, add the chopped parsley and stir well.

3. Serve the prawns in glass bowls.

Tuna steaks and couscous

SERVES: 2 | PREPARATION TIME: 10 MINUTES | COOKING TIME: 7–10 MINUTES

Couscous salad goes well with fish because it is light but full of flavour.

Ingredients

juice 1 lime
1 tablespoon soy sauce
2 garlic cloves, peeled and finely chopped
2 fresh tuna steaks
1 tablespoon oil

For the couscous

1 cup couscous
1 small onion, peeled and finely chopped
2 tomatoes, chopped small
1 small bunch fresh coriander, chopped

1. Mix the lime juice, soy sauce and chopped garlic in a large bowl.

2. Place the tuna steaks in the bowl and coat with the sauce.

3. Heat the oil in a frying pan, then cook the tuna for 3–4 minutes on each side.

4. In the meantime, put the couscous in a large bowl and cover with boiling water. Add the onions, tomatoes and coriander to the bowl.

5. When the tuna is cooked, halve the couscous and serve with the tuna steaks on top.

Fish cakes

MAKES: 4 **PREPARATION TIME: 30 MINUTES** **COOKING TIME: 35 MINUTES**

These fish cakes are perfect for dipping in sweet chilli sauce as a starter, or you could serve them with a summer salad as a main meal.

Ingredients
1 tablespoon butter
100g fresh cod
2 medium potatoes
1 tablespoon chopped parsley
2 eggs, beaten
salt and pepper
50g breadcrumbs
sweet chili sauce, to serve

1. Preheat the oven to 200°C/gas mark 6.

2. Half fill a medium saucepan with water and place it over a high heat to boil.

3. In the meantime, place one-third of the butter on a large sheet of foil and lay the fish on top. Add 2 tablespoons of water and fold the foil around the cod to make a parcel. Place the parcel on a baking tray and bake for 15 minutes.

4. While the fish is cooking, peel and cut the potatoes into 4 and add them to the boiling water. Leave to cook for 20 minutes.

5. When the fish is cooked, carefully remove it from the foil and flake it into pieces in a mixing bowl. Leave the oven on.

6. Drain the potatoes, return them to the pan and add the remaining butter. Mash until smooth (see page 47).

7. Add the mash to the fish as well as the parsley, half the egg, salt and pepper and mix well.

8. Use your hands to shape the mixture into 4 fish cakes.

9. Dip each fish cake in the remaining egg, then coat it in the breadcrumbs.

10. Bake in the oven for 15 minutes until golden. Serve with the sweet chilli sauce.

COOK'S TIP

Try using tuna or salmon for a different flavour.

Fish pie

SERVES: 2　　PREPARATION TIME: 30 MINUTES　　COOKING TIME: 35 MINUTES

To serve more people, simply double this recipe and use a larger ovenproof dish.

Ingredients
100g salmon fillet
100g white fish
1 tablespoon lemon juice
salt and pepper
100g ready to roll puff pastry
peas, to serve

For the sauce
25g butter
25g plain flour, plus extra for
　　dusting
300ml milk, plus extra for brushing

1. Preheat the oven to 180°C/gas mark 4.

2. To make the sauce, heat the butter in a saucepan over a medium heat. Stir in the flour and use a wooden spoon to mix well to make a smooth paste.

3. Slowly add the milk, stirring all the time until the sauce thickens and coats the back of the wooden spoon. Turn the heat down low and leave to simmer.

4. Remove any skin from the fish and cut it into cubes. Add the lemon juice and mix well.

5. Add the cubed fish to the white sauce and season to taste. Stir well and remove from the heat.

6. On a floured work surface, roll out the pastry to a slightly larger shape than the ovenproof dish.

7. Place the fish and sauce in the dish and cover with the rolled pastry. Trim around the edges of the dish to remove any excess pastry. Brush the pastry with a little milk.

8. Bake the pie in the oven for 20 minutes until golden. Serve with cooked peas.

COOK'S TIP

If you do not like salmon, you can replace it with any white fish.

Thai prawn curry

SERVES: 4 **PREPARATION TIME: 10 MINUTES** **COOKING TIME: 10 MINUTES**

With a cooking time of about 10 minutes, this is quick and easy food at its best!

Ingredients
1 tablespoon vegetable oil
500g cooked tiger prawns
1 onion, peeled and finely chopped
1 garlic clove, peeled and finely chopped
2 teaspoons Thai green curry paste
200ml coconut milk

1. Heat the oil in a wok over a medium heat.

2. Add the prawns, onion, garlic and curry paste and fry for 3 minutes.

3. Add the coconut milk and cook for a further 5 minutes. Serve hot.

Spinach and fish bake

SERVES: 4 **PREPARATION TIME: 30 MINUTES** **COOKING TIME: 40 MINUTES**

This fish bake is full of flavour. You can use a combination of fish, for example cod, salmon and hake.

Ingredients
500g potatoes, peeled
500g any fresh uncooked fish
450g spinach
1 tablespoon butter
2 tablespoon milk
250g crème fraiche
50g Cheddar cheese, grated

1. Half fill a large saucepan with water and bring it to the boil.

2. Cut the potatoes into quarters. Add them to the boiling water and cook on high until the potatoes are soft.

3. Preheat the oven to 180°C/ gas mark 4.

4. Remove any skin from the fish and cut it into cubes.

5. Cook the spinach in a large pan for 2 minutes – it is not necessary to add oil to the pan.

6. When the potatoes are soft, take them off the heat and mash them with the butter and milk.

7. Place the fish in an ovenproof dish. Cover it with the crème fraiche and the spinach before topping with the mashed potato.

8. Sprinkle the pie with the grated cheese and bake for 30–40 minutes until the cheese is golden.

Glossary

aquaculture — using the sea, lakes and rivers to raise fish and shellfish

bacteria — tiny living organisms; some are helpful in the body, while others can be harmful

braising — cooking slowly with a small amount of liquid in a closed dish

carcass — the dead body of an animal

cereal — the grain that comes from edible grasses, such as rice and oats

couscous — a North African dish of crushed wheat

cured — preserved

escalope — a thin slice of boneless meat

farrowing house — the place where a sow gives birth to piglets

fibre — the bulky part of food that is needed for digestion

fillet — a boneless piece of meat or fish

free range — raised outdoors

gammon — cured meat from the leg of a pig

intensive farming — raising a large number of animals in a small space

litter — a group of young animals, born at the same time from the same mother

livestock — farm animals, such as cattle, pigs and poultry

marinaded — soaked in a liquid mixture to add flavour

mineral — a substance, such as iron, that is found in the soil and the foods we eat

nutrient — any part of a food that gives the body energy or the goodness it needs to grow

organic — raised without the use of chemicals such as antibiotics, pesticides or preservatives

paté — a spread made from chopped meat or fish and blended with herbs and spices

perishable — likely to rot or go bad quickly

pesticide — a chemical substance that is used to kill pests or weeds

pith — the white tissue than lines the skin of citrus fruits

poached — simmered in a liquid

pot-roasting — braising meat and vegetables with a little water in a covered pot

preservative — a chemical substance that is added to food to make it last longer

preserve — to make food last longer by adding chemicals or using methods such as salting, pickling or smoking

processed food — treated or pre-prepared food

protein — a nutrient that helps the body to grow and repair itself

pulses — the seeds of pod-bearing plants such as beans, which can be dried and used as food

saturated fat — a type of fat that is harmful to the body because it builds up in the arteries and causes heart disease

simmering — to gently boil

species — a particular kind of animal

tandoori — cooked on a spit over charcoal in a clay oven

tikka — marinaded in yogurt and spices and cooked in a clay oven

trotter — a pig's foot used as food

vitamin — a special substance found in food, which the body needs in tiny amounts to stay healthy

Food safety

Each year there are about 70,000 food poisoning cases reported in the UK alone. Sticking to some simple rules can help you avoid this and other kitchen dangers.

1. Clean all your work surfaces before you start cooking.

2. If you have long hair, tie it back away from your face.

3. To avoid a serious injury, always wear shoes in the kitchen.

4. Wash your hands well with soap and warm water before you start to cook. Wash them after handling any raw meat, poultry or fish.

5. Read through the recipe you are cooking before you start. Check that you have all the equipment and ingredients that you will need.

6. Check the sell-by dates on all food.

7. Wash all fruit and vegetables under cold running water.

8. When preparing food, keep it out of the refrigerator for the shortest time possible. Generally, you should not leave food out of the fridge for more than 2 hours.

9. Use a different chopping board and knife to prepare meat, chicken and fish from the one you use for preparing fruit and vegetables.

10. Never serve under cooked food, ensure that any meat, fish and chicken is cooked all the way through.

11. Replace used tea towels regularly with clean, dry ones to avoid the spreading of bacteria.

Useful techniques

Dicing
Cut the meat, fruit or vegetable intro strips about 1 centimetre wide, then chop to give you cubes about 1cm in size.

Blanching
Place the vegetables in a saucepan with just enough boiling water to cover them. Keep them in the water for the required time, which will vary depending on the recipe.

Tenderising
Place the meat on a chopping board and, using a meat tenderiser, hit the meat on each side.

Mashing
Use either a fork or a masher to press down to squash the fruit or vegetable. Continue to do this until there are no lumps left.

Peeling tomatoes
Use a sharp knife to make a cross at the bottom of the tomato. Cover the tomato with boiling water and leave to stand for 3 minutes before removing. The skin should peel back from the cross.

Spicing
Place the meat on a chopping board. Using your preferred spices, massage them in to the cut of meat.

 KNOW YOUR FOOD

Useful information
These abbreviations have been used:
ml – millilitre **g** – gram **l** – litre

1 teaspoon = 5 mililitres
1 tablespoon = 15 mililitres

All eggs are medium unless stated.

Cooking temperatures:
To work out where the cooker dial needs to be for high, medium and low heat, count the marks on the dial and divide them by three. The top few are high, the bottom few are low and the in-between ones are medium.

Index

Useful websites

For information on ingredients and cookery techniques, log on to:

http://thefoody.com/basic/index.html or
http://www.bbc.co.uk/food/glossary

For step-by-step video guides to cookery techniques, log on to:

http://www.waitrose.com/food/cookingandrecipes/cookinglibraries/howtovideos.aspx

For recipes for every occasion as well as tips for planning menus, log on to:

http://www.bbc.co.uk/food/recipes/

FOOD & HOW TO COOK IT!

Contents of titles in series:

WAYLAND